Fri
Hour   rary

S0-ARW-620

smart investing
@ your library®

A partnership between American Library Association
and FINRA Investor Education Foundation

ALA American Library Association

FINRA Investor Education FOUNDATION

FINRA is proud to support the American Library Association

Saving Money

By Dana Meachen Rau

Reading consultant: Susan Nations, M.Ed., author/literacy coach/consultant

Gareth Stevens
Publishing

Please visit our Web site www.garethstevens.com. For a free color catalog of all our high-quality books, call toll free 1-800-542-2595 or fax 1-877-542-2596.

Library of Congress Cataloging-in-Publication Data

Rau, Dana Meachen, 1971–
    Saving money / by Dana Meachen Rau.
      p. cm. — (Money and banks)
    Includes bibliographical references and index.
    ISBN: 978-1-4339-3387-5 (pbk.)
    ISBN: 978-1-4339-3388-2 (6-pack)
    ISBN: 978-1-4339-3386-8 (library binding)
——1. Saving and investment—Juvenile literature. 2. Children—Finance, Personal—Juvenile literature. I. Title. II. Series.
    HB822.R38   2005
    332.6'083—dc22   2005042219

New edition published 2010 by
Gareth Stevens Publishing
111 East 14th Street, Suite 349
New York, NY 10003

New text and images this edition copyright © 2010 Gareth Stevens Publishing

Original edition published 2006 by Weekly Reader® Books
An imprint of Gareth Stevens Publishing
Original edition text and images copyright © 2006 Gareth Stevens Publishing

Art direction: Haley Harasymiw, Tammy West
Page layout: Michael Flynn, Dave Kowalski
Editorial direction: Kerri O'Donnell, Barbara Kiely Miller

Photo credits: Cover, p. 1, back cover © Jayme Thornton/Stone/Getty Images; p. 4 © Riitta Supperi/Gorilla Creative Images/Getty Images; pp. 5, 6, 8, 9, 10, 12, 13, 14, 19 Gregg Andersen; pp. 11, 15, 20, 21 (car and football) Diane Laska-Swanke; pp. 17, 20 (ice cream and basketball), 21 (book) © Shutterstock.com.

All rights reserved. No part of this book may be reproduced in any form without permission in writing from the publisher, except by a reviewer.

Printed in the United States of America

CPSIA compliance information: Batch #WW10GS: For further information contact Gareth Stevens, New York, New York at 1-800-542-2595.

Table of Contents

Boldface words appear in the glossary.

Making Money

A grown-up earns money by working at a job. You might earn money, too. What did you do to help around the house this week? Did you help your dad in the yard? Did you clean your room? Did you do the dishes after a meal?

Mowing lawns is a good way to earn your own money.

Some children get an **allowance**. An allowance is money that is given to a child every week or every month. Children may get paid for helping with jobs around the house. Some parents give an allowance so their children can learn how to **spend** and **save** money.

Some children get an allowance each week.

Did you ever earn money by having a lemonade sale? On a hot summer day, you could probably sell a lot of lemonade. Let's say you charge twenty-five cents a cup. If you sold twenty cups, how much money would you earn? You would earn five dollars.

If this girl sells a lot of lemonade, she will make a lot of money.

A relative might send you a **check** for your birthday. A check is a type of money, too. It is a special slip of paper that you can take to a bank. At the bank, you trade the check for money you can save or spend.

RUBY JOHNSON 1234 PLEASANT ST. MY CITY, USA 12345	12-3456/7890 01234567	1000

DATE *May 25, 2009*

PAY TO THE ORDER OF *Anna Johnson* $ *10.00*

Ten and 00/100 ————   DOLLARS

State Bank

MEMO *Happy Birthday!*   *Ruby Johnson*   MP

⑈ 123456789 ⑈ ⑆ 12   34 5678 ⑈   1234

Some adults give checks to people as gifts for birthdays or other special days.

Save It for Later

There is a lot you can do with the money you earn. You can spend it. If you get a three-dollar allowance, you could buy a toy or a book at the store. You could buy a drink or a treat from a snack bar. Remember to tell an adult before you spend your money.

You can spend your money on things you really want.

You can also save your money. When you save money, you put it away to spend later. When you spend your money right away, you can buy things that cost only as much money as you have. When you save your money, you can buy things that cost more.

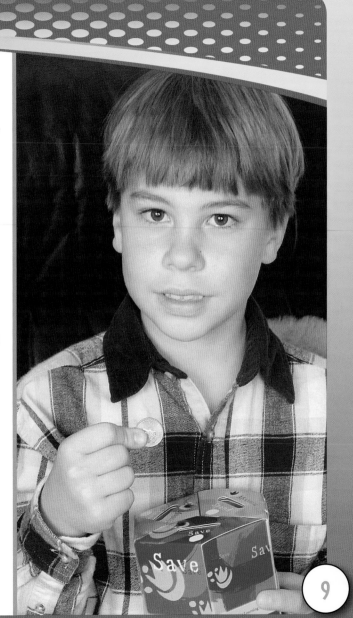

The more money you save, the more you will have to spend later.

Some children save their money for a long time. You can save to buy a game or toy that costs a lot of money. You might even save money to help pay for college.

You might be able to buy a bike if you save your money.

Using two jars helps you keep some money to spend now and save some money to spend later.

You can spend and save at the same time! You can keep your money in two jars. You can label one jar "spend" and the other jar "save." When you earn money, you can put half in one jar and half in the other. What would you like to buy? Would you need to save your money to buy it? It may seem hard to save, but you will be happy you did!

Keeping Money Safe

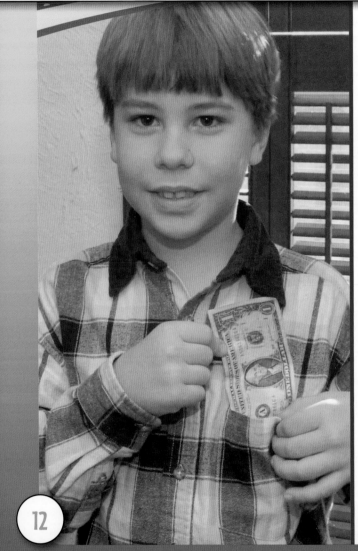

Where do you keep your money? If you keep it in your pocket, you can lose it. You might forget the money is there. The money could fall out or get lost when you wash your clothes. Can you think of a safer place to keep your money?

Always check your pockets before washing your clothes.

When you go to a store, you can keep your money in a wallet. At home, you can keep it in a bank in your room. It is fun to count money to see how much you have saved.

You can sort your money by the kinds of coins and bills you have. The different piles will help you count your money.

A bank in your town or city is another good place to save your money. A parent can help you open a **savings account** at the bank. When you open a savings account, you get a **bankbook**. This little book helps you keep track of how much money you have in the bank.

You can add the amount of money you put in the bank. You can subtract the money you take out.

Make Your Money Grow

Have you ever heard the saying "Money does not grow on trees"? This saying reminds people they need to earn money and save it. It is true that money does not grow like a plant. However, the amount of money you have can grow when you put it in a bank!

A bank is a safe place to keep your money.

When you open a savings account, you are letting the bank use your money until you want it. The bank puts a little extra money in your account to thank you. This extra money is called **interest**. Some banks pay you interest each month. The longer you keep your money in the bank, the more interest the bank gives you.

SAVINGS REGISTER

DATE	DESCRIPTION OF TRANSACTION	WITHDRAWAL	DEPOSITS & INTEREST	BAL. BR'T F'R'D	✓	$75.00
9/15	Allowance		$5.00	AMOUNT OF TRANSACTION		+ $5.00
				BALANCE		$80.00
10/1	Interest		$1.00	AMOUNT OF TRANSACTION		+ $1.00
				BALANCE		$81.00
				AMOUNT OF TRANSACTION		
				BALANCE		
				AMOUNT OF TRANSACTION		
				BALANCE		
				AMOUNT OF TRANSACTION		
				BALANCE		

The interest the bank pays you is added to your savings account.

You can go to the bank to see how much interest you have earned. You can write the amount in your bankbook. Some banks will mail you a note that shows the amount of interest you have earned. Some people use a computer to look at their bank accounts.

You can use a computer to keep track of your savings account.

Investing is another way to save money. Your parents can help you invest. You can buy part of a company! The part you buy is called **stock**. If the company makes money, you do, too. If the company does not make money, then you do not make money either.

When you buy stock, you may get a stock certificate. It shows how much stock you bought.

COMMON STOCK

COMMON STOCK

NUMBER
0123

20

SEE REVERSE SIDE FOR CERTAIN DEFINITIONS

This Certifies that

Anna B Johnson
1234 Pleasant St.
My City, USA 12345

is the record holder of 20

FULLY PAID AND NON-ASSESSABLE SHARES OF CLASS A COMMON STOCK $.01 PAR VALUE, OF

STEELWOLF INC.

transferable only on the books of the Corporation by the holder hereof in person or by a duly authorized attorney upon surrender of this certificate properly endorsed. This certificate is not valid until countersigned by the Transfer Agent and registered by the Registrar.

A statement in full of all the designations, preferences, qualifications, limitations, restrictions, and special or relative rights of the shares of each class authorized to be issued, will be furnished by the Corporation to any shareholder upon request and without charge.

WITNESS the facsimile seal of the Corporation and the facsimile signatures of its duly authorized officers.

Dated JANUARY 13, 2010

TOTALLY GENERIC
SEAL

You never know what you might want to spend your money on in the future. In the meantime, you can keep your money safe. You can watch your money increase until you are ready to spend it on something special.

If you save money, you will always have some when you need it.

Math Connection: Save It Up!

Let's say you get an allowance of two dollars and fifty cents ($2.50) each week. How many weeks do you need to save up for the following items? Find the answers on page 23.

1.

2.

$2.50

$15.00

3.

•$5.00

4.

•$10.00

5.

•$7.50

Glossary

allowance: money that is given at regular times or for a specific purpose

bankbook: a small book that shows money put into or taken out of a bank account

check: a special slip of paper that can be traded for cash or used to pay for something by the person whose name is written on it

interest: money that is paid or charged for the use of borrowed money

investing: buying part of a company; using money to earn interest or make more money

save: to keep for use at a later time

savings account: an account at a bank on which interest is paid

spend: to pay money for something

stock: part ownership of a company

For More Information

Books

Harman, Hollis Page. *Money Sense for Kids.* Hauppage, NY: Barron's Educational Series, 2006.

McGillian, Jamie Kyle. *The Kids' Money Book.* New York: Sterling, 2004.

Minden, Cecilia. *Saving for the Future.* Ann Arbor, MI: Cherry Lake Publishing, 2007.

Web Sites

The Banking Kids Page
www.bankingkids.com/pages/elem.html
Learn how to put money into a savings account

Planet Orange
www.orangekids.com
Learn about making, saving, and spending money

Publisher's note to educators and parents: Our editors have carefully reviewed these Web sites to ensure that they are suitable for students. Many Web sites change frequently, however, and we cannot guarantee that a site's future contents will continue to meet our high standards of quality and educational value. Be advised that students should be closely supervised whenever they access the Internet.

Math Connection Answers: 1. 1 week 2. 6 weeks 3. 2 weeks 4. 4 weeks
5. 3 weeks

Index

About the Author

Dana Meachen Rau is an author, editor, and illustrator. She has written more than one hundred books for children, including nonfiction, early readers, and historical fiction. She lives with her family in Burlington, Connecticut.

332.6 R 2010   HKASX
Rau, Dana Meachen,
Saving money /

KASHMERE GARDENS
08/10